D0758014

CALGARY PUBLIC LIBRARY

OCT   2010

COAL DUST KISSES

ALSO BY WILL FERGUSON

FICTION
Spanish Fly
Happiness™

TRAVEL MEMOIRS
Beyond Belfast
Hitching Rides with Buddha
Beauty Tips from Moose Jaw

HISTORY/HUMOUR
Canadian History for Dummies
How to Be a Canadian (*with Ian Ferguson*)
Why I Hate Canadians

AS EDITOR
The Penguin Anthology of Canadian Humour

AS SONGWRITER
Lyricist for the songs
"Con Men and Call Girls, Part One,"
"Losing Hand," and
"When the Carnival Comes to Town,"
on the Tom Phillips *Spanish Fly* album

WILL FERGUSON
COAL DUST KISSES

A
CHRISTMAS
MEMOIR

VIKING
CANADA

VIKING CANADA

Published by the Penguin Group

Penguin Group (Canada), 90 Eglinton Avenue East, Suite 700, Toronto, Ontario,
Canada M4P 2Y3 (a division of Pearson Canada Inc.)

Penguin Group (USA) Inc., 375 Hudson Street, New York, New York,
New York 10014, U.S.A.

Penguin Books Ltd, 80 Strand, London WC2R 0RL, England
Penguin Ireland, 25 St Stephen's Green, Dublin 2, Ireland (a division of Penguin Books Ltd)
Penguin Group (Australia), 250 Camberwell Road, Camberwell, Victoria 3124,
Australia (a division of Pearson Australia Group Pty Ltd)
Penguin Books India Pvt Ltd, 11 Community Centre, Panchsheel Park,
New Delhi – 110 017, India
Penguin Group (NZ), 67 Apollo Drive, Rosedale, North Shore 0745, Auckland,
New Zealand (a division of Pearson New Zealand Ltd)
Penguin Books (South Africa) (Pty) Ltd, 24 Sturdee Avenue, Rosebank,
Johannesburg 2196, South Africa
Penguin Books Ltd, Registered Offices: 80 Strand, London WC2R 0RL, England

First published 2010
1 2 3 4 5 6 7 8 9 10 (RRD)
Copyright © Will Ferguson, 2010

Illustrations by Marie-Eve Tremblay, colagene.com
Interior design by Mary Opper

All rights reserved. Without limiting the rights under copyright reserved above,
no part of this publication may be reproduced, stored in or introduced into a
retrieval system, or transmitted in any form or by any means (electronic, mechanical,
photocopying, recording or otherwise), without the prior written permission of both
the copyright owner and the above publisher of this book.

Printed in Mexico

LIBRARY AND ARCHIVES CANADA CATALOGUING IN PUBLICATION

Ferguson, Will

Coal dust kisses : a Christmas memoir / Will Ferguson.

ISBN 978-0-670-06916-3

1. Ferguson, Will--Travel. 2. Authors, Canadian (English)--20th

century--Biography. I. Title.

PS8523.E15Z463 2010   C818'.5209   C2010-903079-6

Visit the Penguin Group (Canada) website at **www.penguin.ca**

Special and corporate bulk purchase rates available;
please see **www.penguin.ca/corporatesales** or call 1-800-810-3104, ext. 2477 or 2474

For Alex and Alister

Evidence that science doesn't know everything: Science will tell you that the Northern Lights are silent, cherry blossoms have no scent, and the likelihood of Santa Claus actually existing is low, to say the least.

But in each case I can assert the opposite, just as firmly and with something approaching empirical certainty. For I have heard the Northern Lights, caught the scent of cherry blossoms on the wind, and seen the evidence for Santa Claus firsthand—in the mirror, written on my very skin, a faint but undeniable smudge. Christmas, made manifest.

My father's family were whiskered Scotsmen, coal miners who came over to Cape Breton to cut seams through the darkness, who breathed air that was gritty and cold. They burrowed through the wet black earth, eyes and teeth glowing, their youth and health expendable. Sad-eyed pit ponies pulled the coal to the surface, where it was magically transubstantiated into gold. The coal mines of Cape Breton made a very small number of people very wealthy. None of that wealth or good fortune ever seemed to make its way down the mine shafts, though. It was a hard life, often short. And when a cave-in buried three of my grandfather's brothers, he walked away and never looked back.

He found work on the CNR, shovelling fuel into boiler fires, the locomotives consuming the very coal that had almost consumed him. Steel rails that split the Canadian Shield carried him toward an ever-receding vanishing point, hurling him across the open plains like a javelin, the wind whorling through the grasslands, cinders and sparks tumbling out in short-lived firefly bursts—and there was my grandfather, leaning into it, face to the wind, eating air, grinning.

Although a terse man, and by all accounts one laden with a distinctly Scottish melancholy, he couldn't help himself. He grinned his way across a continent, the wind forcing a smile. He had escaped. He had escaped the mines, had escaped the swallowing dark—and yet coal dust remained gnarled in the roots of our family tree nonetheless, like a trace element embedded deep within our DNA.

As he crossed the prairies, the sun lying low across the grasslands, catching fence posts and extending shadows, my grandfather caught a glimpse of red hair. A girl, bent in the fields, pulling beets, hair blowing every which way. Just a glimpse, but it was enough. He jumped off at the next water tower and walked back along the tracks, ten miles or more in the gathering dusk, stopping at each farm he came to. "I'm looking for the girl with the red hair." He found her, and they were married. (Things were simpler back then.)

That was the family legend, anyway. I've always wondered why he wasn't fired for negligence of duty. Instead he was promoted. He worked his way up to conductor, found himself dressed in a natty jacket and dapper cap. (This

was back when men still knew how to be natty and dapper.) The truth of a story has nothing to do with facts. Perhaps he hadn't been fired by the CNR because the engineer he'd abandoned was charmed by the why of it, by the reason my granddad had gone AWOL in the first place. Maybe they had promoted him based solely on that. *A man walks twenty miles along the tracks to find a girl? How could you not reward him?* Either way, my grandfather had found his red-haired lassie.

Not Scottish, but Norwegian. No matter; my grandmother always said the Scots were simply shipwrecked Norwegians. "They were the Vikings who couldn't navigate."

I've never seen the inside of a mine shaft, and thank God I never will. But the groan of the Cape Breton coal mines echoed through the years even so, in part because one of the few possessions my grandfather took with him when he travelled west was a bit of family lore, one nurtured in those very coal mines.

Who do children wait for on Christmas Eve? Father Christmas. And how does he enter homes? Down through chimneys and up through stove pipes, and although he's always depicted as wearing velvet red, spotlessly clean, his travels would have marked him. Travels always do. And as any person—a miner, say—who's dealt with coal knows, if you spend your time crawling through chimneys, you're going to get covered in soot. It gets inside your lungs and grits your eyes, streaks white beards with grey and turns grey beards black. And so it was with Father Christmas. When he tiptoed through houses, late at night, covered in soot, he would stop to kiss the children on the forehead while they lay sleeping, and when they woke on Christmas morning ... coal dust kisses.

Father Christmas was now known as Santa Claus, and the coal mines of Cape Breton were far away, but my dad and his little sister still ran to the mirror on Christmas morning, still stared in awe at the smudges on their foreheads, knowing that something magical had transpired.

Meanwhile, across the mountains and beside the sea, my mother—daughter of a Belfast orphan—was growing up amid the layered green of the Pacific Northwest. Her earliest memories were of living on a houseboat, her father having become a beachcomber to support his family. Later they would settle into a house on Triumph Street, but the sea was always there, breathing its cool mist. My mother remembers fogs so thick she had to blind-walk her way to school, locating the playground by sound rather than sight, following the echoes of laughter and squeals into the yard as cool damp silhouettes appeared and slowly took shape.

While my mother was baby-stepping her way toward school, my father was lost in the dry-bone dust of southern Saskatchewan. And eventually those two weather systems—the wet mists of the West Coast and the powdered winds of the plains—would come together and collide. Over a hat.

My mother, now working as a nurse in Weyburn, Saskatchewan, met a tall drink of a man at a local dance, and when he left he forgot his hat (this was back when men still wore hats). A fedora, crisply creased, casually tossed to one side. My dad came back to retrieve it, and was able to corral my mother in for further conversation. (The fact that his fedora might have been left behind strategically was something that never occurred to my mother until years later, when her cynical children suggested just such a possibility.)

My father was a man of many hats—salesman, sweet talker, smooth walker, pool hall player—but the one he wore most often was that of Itinerant Schoolteacher. Through various twists and turns, he ended up teaching at a remote school in the far reaches of a northern forest. A distant village, leaking smoke, half-hidden beside a wide arc of the Peace River.

I was born there, under the auroras, and along with my assorted siblings I grew up with the Northern Lights as a backdrop. Shimmering curtains of green, soft glowing blues, strangely subdued yellows: they moved like phantoms across the winter skies of my youth. Me? I thought it was boring. I couldn't wait to get away, couldn't wait to chart my own trajectory. Somewhere far to the south, somewhere interesting and exotic. Edmonton, maybe.

To the Cree of my hometown, the Northern Lights were lost souls, the afterglow of lives lived. To scientists they were *aurora borealis*, caused by charged particles entering the upper ionosphere and then circling in toward the magnetic pole—that other pole, that other north, the one where the compass needles point. Not souls, but atmospheric gases. Green and blue being derived from oxygen, purple from nitrogen, and so on. Science also tells us that the aurora borealis are silent, the drama of their solar storms playing out a hundred kilometres or more above the Earth's surface. But scientists also try to tell us that tomatoes aren't vegetables and pandas aren't bears, so what do they know?

The Earth tilts drunkenly on its axis: this much I do know. The world is not round, it's top heavy, throwing the North first toward the sun and then away, creating long days of summer that never really end, the sun sinking toward the horizon but never quite disappearing. The gathering twilight that passes for night. Not quite the Midnight Sun; more like the Midnight Dusk. Playing outside at eleven o'clock at night, reading books by that magic-hour light. Summers were wonderful. But then the world would begin its long loll back the other way and the darkness would swallow the day, the sun only ever peering up above the trees before dropping back down. Children, walking to school in the dark, coming back in the same.

Science insists that the Northern Lights are silent, but I have snow-crunched home under clear winter skies, have stopped, breath haloing around me in ice-crystal clouds, and stood, neck cricked and eyes to the sky, as the cold fire of the Northern Lights cast its glow—and I assure you, they *speak*. They hiss and pop, they crackle like static, whisper like waves. The northern Cree could make them dance. I've seen it: our neighbours whistling low flat notes, rubbing their fingertips lightly together as the auroras jerked and twitched like kites on

a string. As kids, following our neighbours' example, we whistled our own low flat notes and watched the Northern Lights writhe. A dangerous game, that. Bring them down too quickly, too near, and they might reach out, might grab hold, might never let you go.

The North knows two kinds of people: explorers and settlers. Whereas explorers set out, resolute and strong of jaw, settlers are more pliant. Settlers bend, explorers break. More to the point: settlers stay, explorers are only ever passing through.

My father was like a reverse Polaroid, slowly dissolving, losing shape, blurring first around the edges and then in the details. He would show up, hang around restlessly for a while, and then disappear, following the sudden certainty of some new scheme. Later he would return, chastened but still determined not to give in to mere factualities, not to let the real world win. He would vanish for months at a time, then for years, then for ever.

My mother loved the North; it was where her compass always pointed. (I often wondered if maybe she'd held her whistled note just a beat too long one night, had drawn the auroras in just a little too close.) My father's compass, meanwhile, was anything but resolute; it tend ed to spin wildly like a weathervane on gale winds. When he did come home for a visit it was often at Christmas. He would arrive, invariably at night, with a toot of the car horn and a stampede of kids to the front door, a one-man parade, our very own Santa, throwing trinkets this way and that. And much like Santa, his visits were heady but short; his absences vast and long.

Toys don't last; coal dust does. My father's one enduring legacy lay in that smallest of smudges: in the evidence of a stranger who loved us dearly but couldn't stay, a visitor who quietly kissed our foreheads while we lay sleeping. Christmas morning and another stampede of feet toward the washroom mirror. We crowded in, stared in awe and wonderment. *There, right there!* on our foreheads: chimney soot. Proof positive that Father Christmas had been in our home. It was a moment of magic. Magic in both senses of the word: in the sense of childhood wonder, and in the sense of misdirection and sleight of hand as well. *Did Santa Claus exist?* Well, of course! There was the evidence for all to see, as captured in countless yuletide photographs.

Our mother would have gotten a kiss from Santa Claus, but not our dad, and he'd say with a sad, elongated sigh, "I must not have been a good boy this year. It looks like I've fallen on the wrong side of old Nick's ledger once again."

I remember a Christmas morning when our father was there. Mom came downstairs with dozens of coal dust mementos dabbed all over her face. "Wow!" we said. "Santa Claus must really like you!" She didn't seem very happy about it, though. She just gritted her teeth and went to the sink to try (mostly in vain) to scrub the coal dust off her face.

"Just what exactly is going on with you and this Claus fellow?" my father asked her, voice heavy with disapproval.

Over time my father's visits became less and less frequent, and eventually they stopped entirely. We had our Christmases without him, but the coal dust tradition remained. Our albums were stuffed with photos of us lined up, holding back our hair, displaying what looked—to the untrained eye—not unlike bruises. "Our father used to do that to us," I once said, quite innocently, when I was asked about the marks by a lady who'd been thumbing through our photo albums.

"Your father?" she said, aghast. "He did that to you?"

"Yup. Every Christmas. It was a family tradition. His dad used to do it to him." Then, by way of explanation, "They were Scottish, y'see."

By the time my mom came in from the kitchen with tea, the lady was distraught. It's a wonder she didn't dial Child Services right then and there. But, no, we explained. Not bruises, kisses.

"Did'ja know?" I asked her. "That you can control the Northern Lights?" She was new to the North, so I thought I'd help out, give her some useful tips. "You just have to whistle, and rub your fingers like this. But don't let them get too close," I said. "Or they'll steal your soul."

At which point the lady suddenly remembered a pressing engagement and began inching her way to the door.

To those of us in the North, Canada was a southern nation. Canada was where the radio signals came from, the distant distress calls and muffled chatter from far away, out beyond the Earth's curvature. And it wasn't until 1976 that a bucket brigade of television relay towers finally brought the miracle! of television! to our little pocket of the North. I was in grade six and wonder-bound at the sight of it: flickering images falling from the sky.

The Cold War was still underway, with early-warning radar stations paced out along arctic treelines and silos bristling with ICBMs in distant deserts, ready to intercept incoming Communist arsenal. *Intercept? Where?* We often joked (albeit nervously) that when World War III started our town was where the missiles would land. Which is why I panicked on our first Christmas, P.T. (post television), when the announcer cut in to say that NATO was tracking a mysterious figure coming in across the North Pole. Elsewhere that might have been funny, but when you live on an intercontinental missile path that leads directly across the pole it's not quite as comic as the TV producers may have thought. I bolted upstairs, flinging myself under the bed (thereby protecting myself from certain annihilation), only to hear the announcer chuckle and tell us they'd received a message from the pilot of the unidentified craft that had entered our airspace. *"It reads ... Ho Ho Ho."*

Ho ho ho, indeed. It's a wonder the Americans didn't scramble jets and take down jolly St. Nick right then and there.

Darkness, thick in the trees. Long trudges to the outhouse under undulating skies. Winter rolled on and on, and so did the Northern Lights, in ripples and folds. We continued to whistle, continued to crick our necks skyward. But correlation is not causation, and you reach an age when you stop believing you can make the Northern Lights dance. And that's the same moment they no longer do.

One regret (among many): Memories of my mother asking if I wanted to come with her to a Cree tea dance. There would be drumming and tea (of course) and a circle of dancers shuffling along in moccasins. I rolled my eyes—*God, how lame*—and said no. Every time there was a tea dance she would ask me, and every time I would say no, until finally she stopped asking.

Just as well. I couldn't think of anything more boring than a Native tea dance. I would stare through my own reflection in the bedroom window, would stare at the weight of snow outside. I would conjure up jungles and distant cities, spice islands and saffron seas. I would watch the now-silent Northern Lights, would dream of escape.

I wanted to be anywhere but here. It never occurred to me that my here was someone else's exotic "other."

When I was nineteen I decided to Do Good. I decided to go out into the world, find people less fortunate than I, and Do Good to them. I joined an overseas volunteer corps—though I do confess, my altruistic motives may have hidden a baser motive: to travel far, far away.

My particular group was sent to South America, to the village of Malacatos in the borderlands of Peru on the high Andean heights of Ecuador—a nation named in honour of an imaginary line that runs through it. The equator is the world's balance beam, the bubble in the level, where the days never really lengthen or shorten but remain in the same ratio of darkness and light. I found that fascinating: a world that wasn't off-kilter.

A night flight into Quito, and a twenty-four-hour bus ride through overspills of jungle and past perilous, sheer-drop cliffs, on a road climbing upward into the clouds themselves, a road constantly twisting back on itself—almost meeting itself at times, it seemed—as the air grew thinner, clearer. Our bus was overloaded as any burro, colourful as any rooster. Several of us climbed up top, rode the wind, eating air, grinning. Entanglements of vines and swaths of broad banana leaves, cymbal crashes of colour, waterfalls of flowers, the caw and cry of birds, forests a vigorous green. Condors in holding patterns, coasting on updrafts, carving slow circles in the air. Shadows, moving across distant hills.

The volunteer corps I'd joined sent bands of young Canadians abroad every year, and each group was composed to reflect Canadian society as a whole, with the same ratio of West to East, French to English, rural to urban. Income levels, ethnicity, regional identity: it was all carefully compiled. Each volunteer corps group was, in essence, a mini-Canada, and wherever we went the Ecuadorians would ask us to do—and I quote—"a Canadian dance." The sort of dance that we, as a people, might break into spontaneously at weddings or festivals. Proud Canadians that we were, we made one up. We invented a dance (on your behalf), an awkward version of a square dance with much whooping and clapping, accompanied by random verses of "Alouette" and the occasional failed Ukrainian shupka leap. It was, although not perhaps in the manner intended, quite entertaining for those who watched. Occasionally, as we worked our way with grim resolve through another rendition of our Canadian Dance, we would see the Ecuadorians lean in and whisper to each other. We couldn't hear it, but we knew what they were saying. They were saying, *"Don't say anything. It's their culture."*

Paired up with Ecuadorian counterparts our own age, we were assigned various projects in and around the village of Malacatos, in schools and medical centres, on irrigation projects and sugarcane farms. I stayed with a local family: a mom and dad and three kids, aged four, five, and six ("a good poker hand," as the father said). The mother was boisterous, breathless; she found my very existence amusing, teaching me the local Spanish dialect and roaring with laughter at my efforts, dousing me with water whenever she thought I looked too sweaty and then dusting me with flour when she thought I looked too pink. She, apparently, had never seen a proper towel-snap before. After wiping off from her latest ambush I would chase her around the table while her long-suffering husband looked

on. "Counting my wife, I have four children," he would say, with the resigned sigh of a man who's given up on ever reforming a lost cause.

I'd go swimming in a clear running stream just outside the village, where kids would swing, Tarzan-like, from vines. My fish-belly body always stopped them in mid-swing, the children hanging frozen in air, cartoon-like, as they gaped unabashedly. *Could anybody be that pale?* I tried to explain the unfortunate congruence of Irish, Scots, and Scandinavian that had left me almost without pigment, but it was no use. I was *El fantasma*. "The ghost."

Christmas in Malacatos. A religious procession, late-night Mass, small gifts exchanged. The same growing excitement: *How many nights, Papa? How many nights now?* A green Christmas, humid and lush. The children went to bed late on Christmas Eve, full of yawns and sleepy-eyed protestations that they weren't tired, not at all. I sat up with the father, shared a tumbler or two of *aguardiente*. We talked about how the holiday was observed back where I was from, the similarities and the differences. Earlier I'd told the children that Santa might have followed me down, and they'd strung up socks on the clothesline so that he might drop small gifts in. Nothing from me, you understand. It would be from the Man in Red.

As the kids lay sleeping in that equatorial night, I mentioned to their father the coal dust messages of my own youth, the smudged kisses, and he tilted his head, thinking. Later, under a heavy moon, I staggered out toward the toilet and ran into him in the yard. I'd already placed Santa's gifts in the stockings. (Santa seemed to shop at the local store, having left the same pinwheels, toy flutes, and balsa-wood airplanes as were readily available in Malacatos.) The father smiled at me and raised a finger to his lips. In his other hand he had a small nub of charcoal.

Children are children, and magic is magic. When the Santa Claus kisses were pointed out to the kids the next morning they ran thundering to the nearest mirror with the same galloping energy my siblings and I had shown when we were young. *A visitor had passed through in the night, had left his mark, however small.*

When I said goodbye to Malacatos the children hugged me tight, holding on as though they might stop me from leaving. The father shook my hand in a manly sort of way and the mother cried and cried. The coal dust kisses would remain, though. They would become part of their family's own lore, woven into the holiday, undoubtedly baffling anthropologists for years to come. *"In this one valley, in this one region, in this one corner of Ecuador ..."*

Toronto, the following year. An empty university dorm on Christmas Eve. Calling my mom up North and having our conversation interrupted by a statement one rarely hears in the city: "Hang on, Billy. There's a lynx on the roof." She'd looked out the window while we were talking and had seen a wildcat padding silently across the top of the porch, stalking our dog, Meeko, who was tethered in the yard not unlike a sacrificial offering. And there was my mom, grabbing a broom. "Just a sec," she said. This was followed by the sound of a door opening, a loud thwack, and a "Scat!" It was Mom vs. the Wild, but I wasn't worried. The Wild never had a chance.

She came back on the phone, out of breath. "Scared him off," she said. She'd taken Meeko inside as well, just in case the lynx returned. The poor dog couldn't stop shaking.

On the phone on Christmas Eve, connected tenuously to the North, lying to my mom when she asked if I had somewhere to go, riding the subway in and out of tunnels, keeping myself in motion, staring through my own reflection.

I left Toronto, moved to southern Japan. *Moniyaw! Gringo! Gaijin!* It seemed I'd spent half my life as a stranger in someone else's land. I was now living on the Amakusa Islands amid miniature landscapes and patchwork paddies, the earth the scent of incense. Buddhist temples with wooden joinery that fit together like a puzzle. Shinto shrines with clouded mirrors and torii-gates: rooster perches of the gods. It was a land layered in a lacquer of history and myth. Bullet trains. Samurai castles whose walls rose up like waves about to break. Nothing was ever discarded, it seemed, but rather added on like another coat of shellac.

Case in point: Christmas. I'd heard apocryphal tales of a crucified Santa above Tokyo department store displays, but I highly doubted this. It smacked of urban legend. Still, the yuletide season in Japan was a bit surreal. Though the holiday wasn't officially celebrated, its trappings were understood by most people. And so, in my local neighbourhood noodle house, I would hear the Little Drummer Boy *pa-rum-pa-pum-pumming* on the radio as I slurped my way through an eel and seaweed broth.

Other additions were purely Japanese. Christmas cake, for example. Or the Japanese tradition of Christmas Eve as a time for lovers to spend together, preferably at a romantic inn. Burgeoning relationships were often consummated on Christmas Eve in Japan, something I'm convinced was started by Japanese men. ("But honey, it's a *tradition* ...") The cakes made more sense. I'm not talking about those slabs of fruitcake that circulate uneaten back home. I mean actual birthday cakes, with frosting and sugar swirls.

"Christmas is sort of a birthday, right?" This was how it was explained to me when I asked.

Now, if North Americans attempted to celebrate the Japanese Festival of the Dead or tried to mark National Respect for the Aged Day, I'm sure we would get things muddled up as well. But still. Birthday cakes and lovers' trysts were, I assured them, most certainly not the way one celebrated the yuletide sanctity of Christmas.

And how should one celebrate it?

Well ...

One's own traditions never sound sillier

than when you try to explain them to someone from a different cultural milieu, ever notice that?

"Well," I said, "you need to spend lots of money you don't really have on presents you don't really want. And to truly get into the spirit of the holidays, you need to find the largest turkey known to man and spend the next three days cooking it."

Three days?

"Approximately. Times vary. You will then spend a month and a half gnawing on its carcass until you are so thoroughly sick of turkey that you never want to see it again as long as you live—or until next Christmas, whichever comes first."

"Making yourself sick on turkey is a Canadian tradition?" my Japanese colleagues asked, a touch of incredulity creeping into their voices.

"Yes. You should eat until your belt snaps and gravy is oozing directly out of your pores."

That was nothing. You should have seen their faces when I explained the concept—and process of—"stuffing." *You put it where?*

The coal dust was different, though. That

garnered another sort of reaction. I was living with a Japanese family in a beautiful home with tatami mat floors and a bamboo grove behind. The youngest son, just entering grade three, wanted to know if Colonel Sanders and Santa Claus were the same person, or just related.

"Distant cousins," I said.

"Is he real?"

"No," I said. "He's just a"—I looked the word up—"a myth. He's *based* on a real person. But now he's just used to sell product." Colonel Sanders, that is. As for Santa, I told them stories about coal dust and chimneys and the midnight visits of St. Nick. "I saw it firsthand," I said, pointing at my forehead. "Right there."

Does Santa Claus exist? Only one way to know for sure ...

Christmas Eve, a dab of coal, and another group of kids waking up, running down the hall. *Santa must have followed Will-san to Japan!* The older daughter was dubious. The youngest boy, though, was delighted. He stared into the mirror, saw it with his own eyes. The evidence of something more.

I encountered a rather bemused response to Christmas traditions later on, after I moved from the Amakusa Islands to the mainland of Kyushu. There I'd met a lovely young woman by the name of Terumi, who, through an obvious defect in judgment, had chosen to spend most of her time with me. Terumi had taught English, and had a fairly good grasp of the oddball collage that is Western culture. When Christmas rolled around, though, she asked me about Christmas trees. I had a paper one in my apartment, but I assured her that back home the preferred trees were real. (My dad used to go out on Crown land and saw one down every December. Not until years later did I realize that was illegal.)

"But why a tree?" she asked.

"Well," I said. "They're *evergreens*; they symbolize everlasting life. So we hack one down, drag it inside, and cover it with cheap tinsel."

"What do you do with the tree when Christmas is over?"

"We throw it out."

"In the garbage?"

"Um, yes, but we do it with great reverence."

"Hmm," she said, clearly having her doubts. "How did this start?"

"Well," I said. "It dates back to ancient times when people would gather round to celebrate the, um, winter solstice. Or maybe the lunar equinox. I think the Druids were involved. Or maybe the Romans. Anyway, it is a very old and very sacred tradition."

"You don't know, do you?"

"Not *per se*." (When in doubt, use Latin.)

There was a long pause. "I see."

"It's a tradition," I said, getting a bit huffy. "It doesn't have to make sense."

In the spring, I was stopping by Terumi's house to pick up some oranges her mom had offered me when I noticed that the entrance of their home, like those of offices and shops around town, was decorated with boughs of young bamboo and folded twists of paper.

"It's for Tanabata," Terumi explained. "It's from a story about two lovers who live in the sky. They're separated by the Milky Way. This is the only night of the year they can meet, and only if the skies are clear."

"That's beautiful," I said. "But why the little slips of paper? And why bamboo?"

"It helps the two lovers reunite."

"How?"

"It just does," she said firmly.

"But that doesn't make any sense. I mean, why would—"

"It's a tradition," she said. "It doesn't have to make sense."

There was a long pause. "Hmm," I said.

My own attempts at attaining a Zen-like appreciation of Japanese culture usually fell flat: I could never sit still long enough to float into nothingness, could never stay awake long enough to get all the way through a Noh play. (Something the Japanese themselves often have trouble with. They tend not to snore as loudly as I do, though, or drool quite as conspicuously.) But I did try my hand at haiku, that aphoristic poetic form meant to resonate in one's mind like the leap of a frog breaking the surface illusions of one's existence. I took a certain workmanlike approach to it. I knew that every haiku is required to have at least one seasonal reference, as well as a five-seven-five form. To that aim, I focused my energies, working late into the night, to achieve what would be haiku at its purest, at its most elemental—the haiku as it exists in the Mind of

God, as it were. Here's what I came up with:

SEASONAL REFERENCE
a haiku by Will Ferguson

First, five syllables—
And then, seven syllables.
And now ... back to five.

I recited my masterpiece, my *magnum opus ne plus ultra*, if you will, to an audience of Japanese high school teachers as they sat beneath a champagne froth of cherry blossoms. It was part of our annual *hanami* party, wherein the fleeting flowers of spring—encapsulating so much that is transient and beautiful in life—are duly honoured and celebrated. Unfortunately, my recitation didn't go over very well. Perhaps it was the esoteric nature of the poem, or perhaps it was the nature of cherry-blossom viewing itself, which involves drinking copious amounts of saké. Either way, my poetic aspirations failed to make the impression I was hoping for (rapturous rounds of applause, tearful smiles, offers of fealty, *et cetera*).

The stillness of Zen having defeated me, I chose motion instead, setting out the following spring to travel with the Sakura Zensen, or "Cherry Blossom Front" as it is known, while it moved across Japan. A wave of flowers cresting from south to north and I would surf it, would hanami my way across Nippon. Most of my trip passed in a stuporous haze, but I can say one thing with certainty: just as the Northern Lights are not soundless, the sakura are not odourless, no matter what science tells us. As the petals scatter and fall, showering down in pale pink, they carry a scent, faint but unmistakable. Perfume so soft it seems more memory than real.

I spent five years in Japan, and I used that archipelago nation as a launching pad for wider forays into Malaysia, Indonesia, Korea, China—journeys I took out of an almost contractual obligation to my younger self. I had kept faith with the reflection in the window, the me that had been backlit by Northern Lights and the boreal night.

I thought I'd slipped free, a Houdini escaping the confines of his country, his family, his self. But we carry our home inside us; it's where the compass needles point. And if home is the magnetic pole of the heart, then all journeys eventually become a circle. This was my meagre, delayed-action Zen epiphany: the realization that you can no more escape your home than you can slip free of your own shadow.

I would often meet other backpackers, other expats, restless travellers trying to lose themselves, trying to find themselves. It made me think of other nights and other travellers, of other lights in the sky. Five Christmases without snow and I knew it was time to come home.

Terumi and I were married in a Shinto ceremony in Kumamoto City, laying a sprig of evergreen on an altar, bowing deeply, reading vows, the groom and kimonoed bride sipping from a shared cup of rice wine—the equivalent of a ring on one's finger.

We moved back to Canada soon afterward. I was nudging the family tree closer to Cape Breton with every tack, it seemed. We first settled in a holiday town on the Bay of Fundy, where the ocean performed its table-cloth parlour trick with twice-daily aplomb, pulling out from beneath dinghies and docks, leaving boats stranded. The tides of Fundy are an implacable force, and the wet winter winds they bring are just as implacable. Terumi had never seen snow before, not like this. Her few memories of snow in southern Japan were of faint flakes melting on contact. In the Maritimes, though, the snow lay heavy and thick, picturesque and crushing in equal parts.

I married one of the few Japanese women I know who isn't enamoured with red-haired Anne. Yet we moved farther east nonetheless, to PEI, where Terumi worked in a hotel and I found a job selling Anne of Green Gables Tours to Japanese tourists, which was, I've always said, about as difficult as selling a glass of water to someone whose hair is on fire. Red hair, red soil, grassy dunes, lighthouse beacons turning. Our PEI sojourn was our last hurrah as an unencumbered couple, though we didn't know it at the time.

Children change everything.

I confess that I'd never really liked babies. Especially newborn babies. They never look you in the eye, they're terrible conversationalists, and—there's no nice way to put this—they look like peeled tomatoes. They're so unconditionally *dependent* …

The nurse moved her wand across Terumi's gelled belly, asked if I wanted to hear the heartbeat.

No. Not really. But you can't say that, can you?

"Just let me set up the monitor," the nurse said, "and then I'll pass it to Dad."

Dad. It was the first time I'd ever heard that word in direct reference to myself. I wanted to yell, *"I have a name, do I not?"* But you can't say that, either.

"The green light indicates a proper recording; if the indicator turns red, however, there's no cause for alarm, it just means that the readings are …" and so on, like a fading voiceover. The nurse handed me some sort of stethoscope. She was saying … something. Her voice sounded oddly distant, as though she were at the top of a well and I were at the bottom.

Honestly? I found the notion of a living being dwelling inside my wife a tad disconcerting. It was like a 1950s horror movie: *The Woman with Two Hearts!*

I leaned in, listened. Nothing. Only static and pops. Then, through all the crackle, a clicking sound. A metronome set at double time. One hundred and forty beats a minute, read the monitor. It was like listening to a hummingbird trapped in your hands. Perfectly normal, the nurse said: one hundred and forty beats was in the correct range. She said babies always have rapid heartbeats. She said it had something to do with metabolism.

But I knew why. I knew the real reason. It wasn't metabolism. That's not why that little heart was beating so fast. It was because it was afraid. Afraid. And excited. And nervous. A tiny Morse code transmission coming in over the wire, tapping out a message to my wife, to me, to the world. "*I'm on my way. Are you ready? I'm on my way. I'm gonna be there soon. Are you ready?*"

A winter child. Maritime snow, thicker now than ever. A peeled tomato named Genki Alexander, "genki" from the Japanese for "lively." When his tiny stump of an umbilical cord fell off like a charred piece of wood, I discovered yet another cultural gap that existed between my wife and me. In Japan, a baby's umbilical cord is symbolic of the connection between mother and child; it is saved, carefully preserved.

"Really?"

Terumi nodded. "My mom still has mine," she said. And then: "Why? What do you do with the umbilical cord in Canada?"

"We, um, we throw it out," I said.

She was horrified. "You throw it out? In the garbage?!"

"Yes," I said. "But we do it in a very reverential way."

Somehow, I don't think she believed me. Even now Alex's tiny cord is preserved in an album, alongside footprints and portraits. "What's this?" people ask when they stumble upon it. "That's the hyphen in Japanese-Canadian," I tell them.

On Alex's first Christmas, my wife caught me sneaking into his room with a burnt matchstick in my hand.

"What are you going to do with that?" she asked.

"I'm going to rub it on our son's face," I said cheerfully. "While he's asleep."

"Hmm," she said.

My wife and I often have markedly different approaches to child-rearing, and when we disagree about something we sit down and discuss it in a calm, respectful manner until it's decided that I'm wrong and she's right. The Santa Claus kisses—once I explained them to her—were another matter, though. She liked the story behind it, the continuity. Coal dust and Christmas cake. Little by little, as all families do, we were adding our own layers of lacquer to the proceedings.

A few weeks later and the Great Ice Storm arrived, sheathing branches and power lines, snapping both like bones. Sparks fountained from relay boxes. The sound of muffled explosions outside, and a sudden plunge into darkness. Terrified, we wrapped our newborn baby in mummy-clothes of blankets, huddled together in the bedroom, watched his breath coming out in soft puffs. Powerless in every sense.

Army helicopters arrived like dragonflies. Soldiers disembarked, began clearing fallen debris. We were rescued by a neighbour with a four-wheel drive and taken to an off-season resort hotel, one that had its own generator, and were plunged just as dramatically into a luxury VIP suite with cumulus pillows and a marshmallowy fireplace.

But I never could put that image out of my head, of bundled blankets emitting small exhalations of steam, of something so unconditionally dependent.

Things I have learned from four-year-olds: We live in an observer-affected universe; identity is a social construct; and Santa Claus is the root of all celebrity culture.

We had followed my grandfather's trail west and had settled in a city of optimism and glass towers. Genki Alex, I soon realized, was a child of Buddha-like wisdom, having evidently mastered the most intricate elements of metaphysical physics even before the age of five. The observer-affected universe of quantum theory, where science and metaphysics converge: Alex had no problem with that. A chocolate Easter egg that rolls out from under a chesterfield in mid-August, for example, can be pounced upon and consumed without consequence *as long as we don't tell Mom.*

I'd been poking around under the chesterfield when I dislodged the forgotten relic of Easters past.

"Don't! You'll get sick!" I yelled—after the fact, of course, there being nothing faster in the time-space continuum than a four-year-old going for a chocolate Easter egg. (If anyone doubts the possibility of matter existing in two places at the same time, they had only to see Alex, across the room from the egg, appearing simultaneously at said egg.)

"I won't get sick," he said, having inhaled the chocolate straight out of its tinfoil wrap. "I won't get sick because Mom's not here. She didn't see."

His mom was at the doctor while all this was going on. Another gelled tummy, another hummingbird heart. A spring baby, this time. (And no, Alex didn't get sick from eating the chocolate egg. If anything, he felt emboldened.)

Identity as social construct. Here's how four-year-olds play: they have a hurried, *ad hoc* meeting at the edge of the playground to decide who they will *be* before charging off in a suitably Leacockian manner. "Remember! I'm Buzz Lightyear. Jett is the green Power Ranger. And Aya is a princess cowboy Pokémon. Let's go!" Never mind that every game immediately devolves into simply running and shrieking; it's one's self-selected identity that's the key. It's not what you do, but who you are when doing it that counts.

Amid the mop-water grey of a cold and miserable November, I tried to convince the other parents at the playground to follow suit. "Okay," I said. "I'm a powerful business magnate! You're a fashion model with a degree in marine biology, and we're on a beach in the French Riviera drinking fine wine. Let's go!"

They stopped making eye contact with me after that, oddly enough.

With the arrival of Yuki Alister—"yuki" from the Japanese for "brave"—our quota of potential philosophical input doubled. Alex

had a little brother to torment and torture,
er, mentor and nurture. At two months of age,
Alister, near as I could tell, favoured a form of
"passive hedonism" over that of Buddhist metaphysics, one that seemed to revolve primarily
around bodily functions. The quality of dia-
lectical discourse did heighten over the years,
though, often of the "Alex started it! He hit
me back!" variety. How would a Zen master
handle the internal logic of that?

On our annual familial trek to the mall
for a Photo With Santa™ (in winter, every-
one hangs out at the mall, even Santa) another
epiphany bobbed, corklike, to the surface of
my consciousness. The root of all celebrity, I
realized, lies in these trips to see Santa. This
is where we learn it, this is where it starts. The
long queue, the trembling excitement, the
carefully choreographed public appearances,
the photographic souvenir, the pleading,
deluded fan letters—the cult of celebrity begins
at Santa's knee, I'm convinced of it.

And yet ...

No matter how tired and cranky, how jaded
or cynical, how utterly *tiresome* Christmas
becomes, there is always a kernel of magic at

the core, isn't there? Sometimes it's present in something as small as a smile, or a carol sung off-tune in the family car, or a single smudge of coal on Christmas morning. Even at age three, Alister understood this. Somehow, he always knew the Santa at the mall was just pretending. But the coal dust? That was real.

The years go by, as they do, and Alex and Alister still wake on Christmas morning to find faint traces of coal on their foreheads. In a connect-the-dots journey across four continents and as many countries, a Scottish coal-mining tradition has gone from Cape Breton to the northwest woods, from Ecuador to southern Japan, and back again to Canada.

An Irish friend of mine once described the four stages of a man's life as follows: believing in Santa Claus, not believing in Santa Claus, *being* Santa Claus, and, finally, looking like Santa Claus. I was edging closer to that final stage with every breath, it seemed.

Alex, at age eight: slowly working things out, like a code-breaker or a safe-cracker, clicking the various pieces of the puzzle into place, not realizing I was part of the conspiracy. "Think about it, Dad," he says, voice hushed, eyes flitting over his shoulder. "How could one person get to so many houses on the same night?"

I lean in, drop my voice to a whisper, too—*Who knows how far this goes?*—"What are you saying, son? That there's some kind of—"

"It doesn't add up," Alex says, using a phrase he learned from Encyclopedia Brown. "All those chimneys, all over the world, *in one night?*"

I stroke my jaw. Frown. "But what about the Santa Claus kisses?"

And it's Alex's turn to frown. That part, he hasn't figured out. But it's coming ... soon.

But not now. Not yet.

anta Claus visits my brother Sean's home in Montreal as well. His daughters and son wake to find coal dust on their foreheads, too, and one Christmas I was complaining to him over the phone about how *early* Santa has to wake up just to catch the little monkeys before they spring out of bed and run to the mirror.

"Santa Claus uses actual coal dust at your house?" Sean asked.

"Um, yeah. Why?"

"Because over here, Santa has figured out that mascara looks a lot like charcoal. And if it's waterproof mascara, it won't smudge the pillows, either. Santa can leave his kiss before he goes to bed and then sleep in, even while his kids are jumping up and down on the mattress shouting *Santa was here! Santa was here!*"

All those years, setting the alarm at some godawful hour, staggering bleary-eyed down the hall to dab a bit of Cape Breton on sleeping children before anyone can— "Mascara?" I said.

"Mascara."

There was a long pause. "Well, well, well," I said. "The Santa at your place must feel pretty friggin' clever."

Sean laughed. "He does."

By the time Alister the Brave entered this world, my father had exited, stage left.

Alister on his grandma's lap, as she reads stories to him that she once read to me. *"Now Sam McGee was from Tennessee, where the cotton blooms and blows..."* His fearless lynx-chasing, West Coast-born, North-enamoured grandma is still going strong, but his grandfather is not. Alister's grandfather has been reduced to a faint smudge, a container of ashes, a collection of contradictory tales and competing testimony. Gone, but not quite.

My father tends to reappear at the strangest of times.

I was at yet another writers' festival, on yet another book panel. The question our esteemed lineup of authors was labouring upon was—wait for it—"Which work would you take with you to a desert island?" The answers, as always, were as interminable as they were disingenuous. *"Proust. And Tolstoy, of course. I find myself revisiting Anna Karenina every year without fail, because I get so much more out of it each time."* Yeah, sure you do.

I sighed, focused my energy on not wandering off, catching a ride to somewhere else. As the question worked its way down the line like a plodding dray horse, it dawned on me that I actually had the right answer, for the first time ever! "Which book would you take with you to a desert island?" When they got to me, I said, *"How to Survive on a Desert Island."* The other panelists thought I was kidding, but no. Forget *Anna Karenina*; I wanted a book that would tell me how to stay alive. "How to spear fish and build a shelter," I said. "How to start a fire without matches, how to signal for help, how to distinguish between edible plants and poisonous ones, that sort of thing."

After the event was over, and the hordes of swooning women who follow authors around had been forcibly dispersed, I was pulling on my jacket when an older lady appeared.

"I knew your father," she said. "You're just like him." Was that a compliment or a critique? Before I could ask her to clarify, she said, by way of explanation it seemed, "You have his eyes." Then someone cut in, someone else asked a question, and the woman folded herself back into the crowd.

I think about that sometimes, about the woman in the crowd and what she might have meant. When I related the incident to my wife, Terumi said, "Maybe she was one of his students." Probably. My dad taught a lot of people over the years.

Alister was more worried about the desert island, though. "Why would you be on an island?" he asked. "And why would you take a book?"

"I don't know. Maybe I was riding in a hot-air balloon and it sprang a leak. Maybe I had the foresight to pack reading material, just in case I landed on a desert island."

Alister's eyes started to fill with tears. "You would be all alone? On an island? Even at night-time?"

"Just a scenario," I said. "A story. It's not really gonna happen, just 'what if.'"

Then, with a sniff and a sudden burst of confidence, he said "You wouldn't be lost. Santa Claus would find you."

It snowed soon after my dad died. Great story-book flakes wafting down and feathering the streets. I went for a long walk. So long, in fact, that I considered the possibility of not turning around, but just walking and walking. By that point the skies had cleared and constellations had appeared, those make-believe maps we project onto the sky. The trick with travelling is knowing when to stop, when to turn around and come back. It was a knack my dad never mastered.

It was well after midnight when I finally made it home, face red and nose numb. My wife woke to ask me, sleepily, where I had been.

"I went out for bit," I said. "I took the long way back, is all."